This book belongs to

Silly Billy!

How do you confuse
a Silly Billy?
Offer him two spades
and ask him to take
his pick.

Why did the Silly Billy
fall out of his window?
He was ironing his curtains.

Did you hear about the
fool who kept on going
round saying no?
Silly Billy: No.

Did you hear about
the Silly Billy who took
up tap dancing?
He fell into the sink.

Did you hear about
the Silly Billy who
swallowed a light bulb?
After he spat it out
he said he felt delighted.

Did you hear about
the Silly Billy who would
plow his field with a
steamroller?
He said he wanted to
grow mashed potatoes.

What did Silly Billy
do when he saw a
sign on a bench saying
wet paint?
He got a bucket of
water and poured it
over the bench.

How does Silly Billy
call his dog?
He puts two fingers in
his mouth and shouts
'Barny!'

Five Silly Billy's have got lost on this page, find them and then colour the page in!

If you've made it look very Wonderful, take a picture and show your friends.

Jokes to tell Teacher

What's a pirates favourite lesson?
Arrrrt!

Why was the broom late for school?
It overswept.

What do elves learn at school?
The elf-abet.

Who invented fractions?
Henry the Eighth.

Did you hear about the boy who took the school bus home? The teachers made home bring it back.

Why did the teacher turn the light on?
Because her class was so dim.

Why did they nose hate school?
He kept getting picked on.

How do bees get to school?
On the school buzz.

How did you find school today?
I just got off the bus and it was there.

Teacher: You aren't paying attention. Are you having trouble hearing?
Pupil: No miss, I'm having trouble listening.

Jokes to tell Teacher

Did you hear about the farmer who won the Nobel prize? He was out standing in his field.

Did you hear about the man who couldn't tell the difference between toothpaste and putty? His windows fell out.

What happened to the two bed bugs who fell in love? They got married in the spring.

How did the car get a puncture? From the fork in the road.

Why did the nose cross the road? Because he was getting picked on.

Surgeon: Just relax, there's no need to worry? Patient: But it's my first operation and I'm really nervous. Surgeon: Well, it's my first operation and I'm not worried at all.

Where does Robbin Hood by his flowers? At Sherwood Florists.

Why did the poet have to get a proper job? Because he realised rhyme doesn't pay.

How easy is it to please a greedy person? It's a piece of cake.

Teacher: What does coincidence mean? Pupil: That's funny, I was just going to ask you that?

Silly Family's

Dad: Why are you home from school so early?
Son: I was the only one who could answer the question.
Dad: Well, done son what was the question?
Son: Who broke the window.

Son: Dad why is your face so wrinkly?
Dad: They're not wrinkles, they're laughter lines.
Son: Trust me, nothing's that funny.

Dad: Why does everyone call you teachers pet?
Son: She keeps me in a cage.

Sister: I look awful in this dress, can someone give me a compliment?
Brother: You have perfect eyesight!

Brother: Whats the difference between a hippos bottom and a postbox?
Sister: I don't know.
Brother: Well, I'd better not give you my letters to post, then.

Brother: What do you mean by telling all your friends I'm an idiot?
Sister: I'm sorry, I didn't know it was a secret.

Son: Mum, can I have another glass of water, please?
Mum: Thats the fifth one since you went to bed, why are you so thirsty?
Son: I'm not thirsty, my bedrooms on fire!

Son: Mum, what's the most dangerous thing about driving?
Mum: The nut behind the steering wheel.

Silly Family's

Why do parents carry their babies?
Because their babies aren't big enough to carry their parents.

Dad: you promised me You'd make 100 per cent effort this week.
Son: I did! Monday 25 per cent Tuesday 35, 15 on Wednesday and Thursday and 10 on Friday!

Why was the toast unhappy after marrying the margarine?
She was expecting someone butter.

Dad: When your grandpa was in the army he saved the whole regiment.
Son: What did he do?
Dad: He shot the cook.

Son: Dad do you have a good memory?
Dad: Yes son why do you ask?
Son: Oh, I broke your shaving mirror.

Dad: Son why didn't you mow the lawn last week?
Son: I broke my leg last week.
Dad: That's a lame excuse.

Sing to Mum!
For she's a jolly good fellow
Her hearts is sweeter Than gello
Her skins as soft as marshmallow
And so say all of us!
And so say all of us!

Daft Jokes!

What do campers need
after a big drink?
A Tea-pee.

What do you call
a baby ant?
An infant.

Who carry's a
big sack and
goes oh, oh, oh?
Sant Claus walking
backwards.

How do you
start a soft
toy race?
Ready, Teddy Go!

Where does a
boat go when
it's sick?
To the dock.

What's the best
time to go to
a dentist?
Tooth-hurty.

What did the duck
say when he fell over
in a China shop.
I hope I didn't
quack any.

What's big and yellow
And arrives early every
morning to brighten
your moms day?
The school bus.

Silly Cat & Mouse

What cat
should you never
play cards with.
A cheetah.

What do cats
eat for breakfast?
Mice-krispies.

How do cats
keep their soda
cold?
With mice-cubes.

What's grey has
four legs and
a trunk?
A mouse going
on holiday.

What do you get
if you cross a
cat with a lemon?
A sourpuss.

What's brown has
four legs and
a trunk?
A mouse coming
back from holiday.

What do cats do
when they buy a
new home?
They celebrate with
mouse warming party

What cat grows in
a garden?
A dandelion.

What did the mouse say when he
broke his teeth?
Hard cheese.

Once you found eight lost kittens, then you can colour in the picture.

Knock, Knock!

Knock, Knock!
Who's there?
Cornflakes.
Cornflakes who?
I'll tell you next week
it's a cereal.

Knock, Knock!
Who's there?
Pudding.
Pudding who?
Pudding your pants
after your trousers is
not a good idea.

Knock, Knock!
Who's there?
Reed.
Reed who?
Reed all about it
a boy opens his door.

Knock, Knock!
Who's there?
Little old lady.
Little old lady Who?
I didn't know you
could yodel.

Knock, Knock!
Who's there?
Duck.
Duck who?
JUST DUCK! There's a
missile coming!

Knock, Knock!
Who's there?
Tamara.
Tamara who?
Tamara I'll use
your window.

Knock, Knock! Who's there?
Mary Lee. Mary Lee who?
Mary-Lee, Mary Lee, life is But a dream.
Row, row , row your boat...

Knock, Knock!

Knock, Knock!
Who's there?
Dawn.
Dawn who?
Dawn just stand there
open the door!

Knock, Knock!
Who's there?
Nadia.
Nadia who?
Nadia business.

Knock, Knock!
Who's there?
Arge and Tina.
Arge and Tina who?
Arge and Tina
just won the cup!

Knock, Knock!
Who's there?
Kay.
Kay who?
Kay sera sera!

Knock, Knock!
Who's there?
Justin.
Justin who.
Justin time, it's
starting to rain.

Knock, Knock!
Who's there?
Abby.
Abby who?
Abby birthday
to you!

Who's there? Joo. Joo who?
Joo-who let the dogs out?

Best Jokes!

Where was grandad when the
lights went out?
In the dark.

Did you hear about the girl
who slept with her head under
her pillow?
The fairies took all her teeth away.

What cowboy lives at the bottom
of the sea?
Billy the Squid.

How did the tap dancer break
his leg?
He fell into the sink.

Where did Napoleon keep his
armies?
Up his sleevies.

Best Jokes!

What happened when the lion
who ate the man?
He felt funny.

Where would you weigh a whale?
At a whale-weigh Station.

What's wrong with a man with
jelly in one ear and sponge in another?
He's a trifle death.

What did Tarzan say when he saw
elephants coming over the hill?
Here come the elephants.

What did the first mind reader
say to the second mind reader?
You're all right how am I?

Best Jokes!

Mum: Why are you crying?
Boy: Dad hit his thumb with the hammer.
Mum: Knowing you I'm surprised you
didn't laugh.
Boy: That's the trouble I did.

What did the earwig say
when he fell off the wall?
Earwig go again.

How does a witch tell the time?
With a witch watch.

Who did Dracula marry?
The girl necks door.

I can make you talk like a
Red indian?
How?
See, I told you.

Cross The Road Jokes

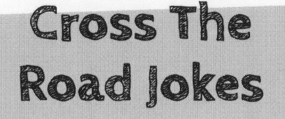

Why did the rooster
cross the road?
To cock-a-doodle-doo something.

Why did the dog
cross the road?
To get out of the barking lot.

Why did the cat
cross the road?
Because it's owner told it
not to do it.

Why did the chicken
cross the road, roll in dirt
and then walk back?
Because it was a dirty double crosser.

Cross The Road Jokes

Why did the germ
cross the lab?
To get to the other slide

Why did the fish
cross the ocean?
To get to the other tide.

Why did the hedgehog
cross the road?
To see his flat mate.

Why did the cow
cross the road?
to get to the udder side.

Silly Pirates

How much do pirate earrings cost? A buccaneer.

Why does it take a pirate so long to learn the alphabet? Because he spends too long at C.

Why did Captain Hook cross the road? To get to the second hand shop.

What lies at the bottom of the ocean and twitches? A nervous wreck.

What's orange and sounds like parrot? Carrot.

Why are Pirates called pirates? Because they aaaarrrrr!

Why couldn't the pirate play cards? Because he was standing on the deck.

What did the pirate name his daughter? Peggy.

What did the dyslexic pirate say? RRRRRRA1

Where can you find a pirate that's lost his wooden leg? Right where you left him.

What's the difference between a hungry pirate and a drunken pirate? One got a rumbling tummy, and the others got a tumbling rummy.

Silly pirate drank to much rum and lost 11 diamonds from his treasure chest. You've ten minutes to find them all, or walk the plank.

Best Jokes!

Did you hear about the cat
that married a glove?
They had mittens.

What's the difference between a wet
day and a lion with tooth-ache?
One's pouring with rain; the other's
roaring with pain.

What goes dot-dot-dot-croak?
Morse toad.

What do you call a hot
sausage in space?
An unidentified fry Object. (UFO).

Two aerials meet on a roof, fall in
love and get married. The ceremony was
rubbish but the reception was fantastic.

What's the hardest part of milking
a gerbil?
Getting the bucket under it.

Best Jokes!

Boy: I think my teacher loves me.
Mum: How can you tell?
Boy: She keeps putting kisses by my sums.

What do you get if you
cross an owl with a skunk?
A bird that smells but doesn't
give a hoot.

The Wally family were driving to
see Stonehenge. They saw a sign saying
'Stonehenge Left'. They were very angry
and drove straight home.

I used to be indecisive-
now I'm not so sure.

'Can you help me?' a worried
man asked the animal shelter officer.
'I'm looking for a stray dog with one
eye.' 'Would it help if you used both
eyes?' yawned the officer.

Silly Books

You'll find these books in a Silly Library.

Coffee maker
by Phil Turr

REMEMBERING ANNIVERSARIES
BY BETTY WONT

Great Breakfast
By Hammond Deggs

Bull Fighting
by Mat Adore

Leaky Boat
By I . C. King

Building Wigwams
By T. P

Long Winter
By Ron. E. Nose

Lovely Breakfast
by Roland Jam

How to keep pigs
By Chris p. Bacon

Life In Prison
By Robbin Banks

Blushing
By Rosie Cheeks

Old School Recording
By Cass Ete

Antibiotics
By Penny Silling

Nosey neighbours
by Annette Curtain

Silly Jobs

Why was the postman fed up?
He got the sack on his first day.

What did they call Postman Pat when he retired?
Pat.

How do you become a professor?
By degrees.

How do greengrocer's mend the holes in their trousers?
With cabbage patches.

Why are train drivers always anxious?
Because their jobs always on the line.

Where do generals keep their armies?
Up their sleevies.

What kind of fish do fishermen catch at night?
Starfish.

Why do surgeons wear masks?
So that if they make a mistake, nobody will know who did it.

What's the most exhausting month to be a soldier?
The month of March.

What happens when the Queen burps?
She issues a royal pardon.

What kind of training do you need to be a waste collector?
None- you just pick it up as you go along.

Silly Riddles

What's hidden in the pictures?

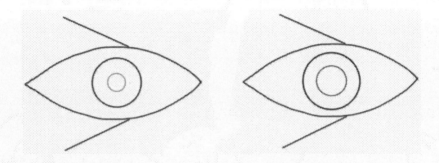

Two Mexicans rowing two boats.

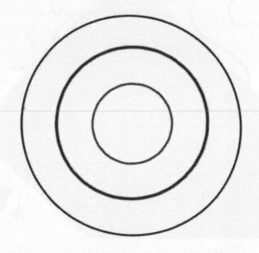

A large Mexican wearing a sombrero.

Silly Riddles

What's hidden in the pictures?

After the python met the zookeeper.

Two men and a vase.

Best Jokes!

Did you hear about the magic tractor?
It went down the lane and turned into a field.

How does an Eskimo build his house?
Igloos it together.

How many ears did Captain Kirk have?
Three: a left ear, a right
ear and a final frontier.

What do you call a camel with
no humps?
Humphrey.
What do you a camel with three humps.
Lumpy.

What did the Martian say to the
petrol pump?
Take your finger out of your ear
when I'm talking to you.

How do you know flowers are lazy?
You always find them in bed.

Best Jokes!

Boy: I think my teacher loves me.
Mum: How can you tell?
Boy: She keeps putting kisses by my sums.

What do you get if you
cross an owl with a skunk?
A bird that smells but doesn't
give a hoot.

The Wally family were driving to
see Stonehenge. They saw a sign saying
'Stonehenge Left'. They were very angry
and drove straight home.

I used to be indecisive-
now I'm not so sure.

'Can you help me?' a worried
man asked the animal shelter officer.
'I'm looking for a stray dog with one
eye.' 'Would it help if you used both
eyes?' yawned the officer.

Best Jokes!

Brother: 'Why are you cutting up that block of ice?'
Sister: 'So that it will fit into the ice cube tray of course.'

Boy: 'Dad what do you do for a job?'
Dad: 'It's very important, I have thousands of men under me.'
Mum: 'Your Dad works in a cemetery.'

Teacher: 'How was your holiday in Switzerland Tom?"Was the scenery lovely?'
Tom: 'It was hard to see the scenery, the mountains kept getting in the way.'

Brother: 'Birthday cake gives me heartburn.'
Sister: 'Try taking the candles off before eating it next time.'

Silly Sea

Why was the mermaid
so bitter?
She grew up with
a ship on her shoulder.

Why do oceans
never go out of
style?
Because they're
always current.

Why did Noah
only catch two fish?
He only had
two worms.

Doctor, Doctor,
I smell like a fish.
Oh you poor sole.

Why was the lobster
sent to prison?
He kept on pinching
things.

Why do fish swim
in salt water?
Because pepper makes
them sneeze.

What fish makes
a goes with ice cream?
A jellyfish.

What day do fish
hate most?
Fryday.

What's a sharks
favourite game?
Swallow the leader.

What do you call a fishes date?
His gill-friend.

What do you call a boats date?
Her buoy-friend.

Silly Sea

When is fishing
not a good way
to relax?
When your a worm.

What did the ocean
say to the shore?
Nothing it just waved.

What kind of fish
can't swim?
Dead ones.

What do you get
if you cross a fish
with an elephant?
Swimming trunks.

How do you
communicate with
a fish?
Drop him a line.

What cats love water?
Octopusses.

What runs but
never walks?
Water.

Why did the oyster
go to university.
Because he had pearls
of wisdom.

Why did the crab
blush?
Because the sea-weed.

How do you chop
waves?
You don't you cut
them in half, with
a sea saw.

Sam: If frozen water
is iced water, what is
frozen ink?
Jim: Iced ink.
Sam: I know you do!

What did the useless fisherman catch?
A cold.
See if you can spot his rod.

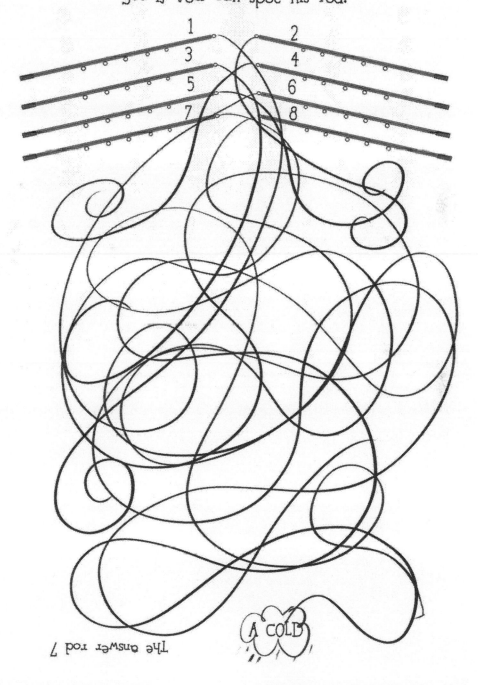

The answer rod 7

A COLD

Find ten seahorse
shadows then colour
In the coral sea!

Knock, Knock!

Knock, Knock!
Who's there?
Pig.
Pig who?
Pig me up at four
and don't be late!

Knock, Knock!
Who's there?
Goat.
Goat who?
Goat to the door,
open it and
you'll see.

Knock, Knock!
Who's there?
Abee.
Abee who?
Abeecd E F G.

Knock, Knock!
Who's there?
Gorilla.
Gorilla who?
Gorilla me a burger,
I'm starving!

Knock, Knock!
Who's there?
Lion.
Lion who?
Lion on the sofa
all day is lazy, open
the door.

Knock, Knock!
Who's there?
Cook.
Cook who?
Cuckoo have you
been eating
bird seed?

Knock, Knock! Who's there? Berry.
Berry who? Berry glad to see you,
NOW LET ME IN!

Knock, Knock!

Knock, Knock!
Who's there?
Mice.
Mice who?
Mice to meet you,
cat you later!

Knock, Knock!
Who's there?
Radio.
Radio who?
Rad-io not,
here I come!

Knock, Knock!
Who's there?
Peas Who?
Peas to meet you,
lettuce in.

Knock, Knock!
Who's there?
Man ooher
Man ooher who?
Man-ooher on your
door step clean it up!

Knock, Knock!
Who's there?
Hawaii.
Hawaii who?
I'm fine, Hawaii you?

Knock, Knock!
Who's there?
Egg.
Egg who?
Egg-cited to
meet you.

Knock, Knock! Who's there? You.
You who? You-who, I'm still waiting.

Waiter, Waiter!

Waiter, What's this fly doing on my ice cream?
Waiter: Looks like it's skiing, Sir.

Waiter, This food is awful!
Please get me the manager!
Waiter: He won't eat it either, sir.

Waiter, there appears to be a dead wasp in m soup.
Waiter: Yes, Sir, they're not very good swimmers.

Waiter, This steak taste funny.
Waiter: Then why aren't you laughing?

Waiter: This coffee taste like mud.
That doesn't surprise me, it was only ground a few moments ago.

Waiter, My wife wants to know if you serve frogs legs?
Waiter: Yes, Sir, tell her to take a seat, we serve anyone here sir.

Waiter, Have you got chicken legs?
Waiter: No, Sir, it's just the way I walk.

Waiter, is there soup on the menu?
Yes, let me wipe it off.

Waiter, you've got your thumb in my soup!
Waiter: Don't worry, Sir it's not very hot.

Waiter, Waiter!

Waiter, what do you call this?
Waiter: It's bean soup, sir.
Man: I don't care what it's been- what is it now?

Waiter: How did you find your steak?
Man: Well I just moved a chip and it was there.

Waiter, will my pizza be long?
Waiter: No, sir, it will be round.

Waiter, this egg is bad!
Waiter: Don't blame me, sir,
I only laid the table.

Waiter, There's a fly on my spaghetti.
Don't worry, sir, that spider on your bread will get him.

Waiter, my plates all wet!
Waiter: That's your soup, sir.

Waiter, I've just found a slug on my salad.
Waiter: Don't worry, sir, won't charge you any extra.

Waiter, why on earth is there a footprint on my steak?
Waiter: You did ask me to step on it, sir.

Waiter: What will you have, sir?
Man: Steak and kiddy pie, please.
Waiter: You mean steak and kidney pie, sir.
Man: I said kiddly, diddle I?

Cross The Road Jokes

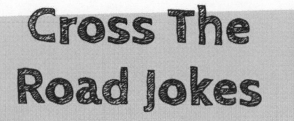

Why did the duck cross the road?
To prove he wasn't chicken.

Why did the turtle cross the road?
To get to the shell station.

What happened when the elephant crossed the road?
He stepped on a chicken.

Why did the chewing gum cross the road?
Because it was stuck on the chickens foot.

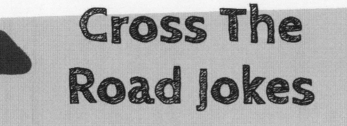

Cross The Road Jokes

Why did the fox
cross the road?

He was following the chicken.

Why did the chicken
cross the road?
Because it was a free range chicken.

Why did the rubber chicken
cross the road?
To stretch its legs.

Why wouldn't the bike
cross the road?
Because it was two-tired.

Guess The Creature?

Strange named creatures!

Blue-footed booby
A bird from Peru.

Laughing jackass
Bird New Zealand.

Pudu
Small deer.

Bongo
Antelope.

Obese Lilly weevil
Beetle.

Purple Grackle
Bird USA.

Golden-rumped tinkerbird
Bird Congo.

Aye-aye
Lemur.

Tiny tuco-tuco
Rodent.

Gang gang cockatoo
Bird Australia.

Aha ha
Wasp.

Spotted thick knee
Bird Ethiopia.

Find six owl heads, then make
this page look beautiful.

Silly Animal Facts

Squirrels plant thousands of new trees
each year by forgetting where they put
their acorns.

Cows can have best friends. Maybe they
go to the moovies together!

The Gentoo penguin proposes to
his life mate with a pebble.
It's less expensive than a gold ring!

Macaques monkeys in Japan, use coins
to buy vending machine snacks.

Puffins mate for life. They make
their homes on cliff sides and
always set aside room for their toilet.

Seahorses mate for life, and when
they travel they hold each others' tails.

Dogs' nose prints are as unique as
human fingerprints and can be used
to identify them.

Crows are so intelligent they can play
pranks on each other.

Butterflies taste with their feet. Yuck!

Silly Animals

Is your dog
fond of children?
Well, yes but he
prefers tinned dog
food.

Why wouldn't the
lady buy a duck
egg?
In case it had a
quack in it.

Why can't you hide
a leopard?
Because he's always
spotted.

How does an
elephant get down
from a tree?
He sits on a leaf
and waits till
autumn.

Hickory dickory dock,
Two mouse ran up
a clock.
The clock struck one
but the other escaped
with minor injuries.

What do you call
a chicken in a
shellsuit?
An egg.

What should you
do if you meet
a blue whale?
Try and cheer
it up.

Why do cows lie
down when it's cold?
To keep each udder
warm.

What's black and white and
red all over?
A penguin falling down the stairs.

Silly Animals

What do you call a cow that lives in an igloo? An Eskimoo.

Why did the farmer call his pig ink? Because he kept on running out of the pen.

Where can you find a cat with no legs? Wherever you left it.

What goes dot-dot-dash-dash-squeak.

What's the best way to catch a squirrel? Climb up a tree and act like a nut.

What do you get if you cross a frog with a ferry? A hopper craft.

What do you call a three legged donkey? A wonkey.

Did you her about the frog who's car broke down? He got Toad away.

What do you call a man with a rabbit up his jumper? Warren.

What time do ducks wake up? At the quack of dawn.

What do you call a camel without a hump? Humphrey.

Silly Animals

Why is a puppy good at DIY? Because he's always doing little jobs around the house.

Why did the pony cough? Because he was a little horse.

What do you call a pig that does karate? A pork chop.

Did you hear about the two birds that fell in love? They became tweethearts.

What's black and white and makes a lot of noise? A penguin with a drum kit.

What do you get If you cross an skunk with an owl? Someone who stinks but doesn't give a hoot.

What bird is always out of breath? A puffin.

What's black and white eats like a horse? A zebra.

How do horses propose? On bended neigh.

Find the 22 hidden fox's in ten minutes!

Silly Riddles

What's hidden in the pictures?

The face of a man and the word liar.

An Elephant leg illusion.

Silly Riddles

What's hidden in the pictures?

A man playing saxophone and a woman.

An Indian and a Eskimo cave.

Doctor, doctor!

Doctor, Doctor,
My eyesight is getting
worse.
It certainly is this
is a chip shop.

Doctor, Doctor,
I've swallowed a
watch.
Don't worry, as
time passes you'll
feel better.

Doctor, Doctor,
I keep thinking I'm
a sewing machine.
Oh, that's funny, you've
got me in stitches.

Doctor, Doctor,
Please help me, I can't
stop shaking.
Do you drink a lot?
Not really I spill
most of it.

A man walks into a
doctors office. He has
a carrot stuck up his
nose, a banana sticking
out of one ear, and a
cucumber sticking out
of the other.
The doctor takes one
look at him an says, "you're
not eating properly."

Doctor, Doctor,
I feel like a very
slow boomerang.
I'll try catch and
you tomorrow.

Doctor, Doctor,
I'm frightened of
squirrels.
You must be nuts!

Doctor, Doctor,
Can you help me out?
Certainly, what way did
you come in?

Why did the clown go to the doctors?
Because he was feeling a little funny.

Doctor, doctor!

Doctor, Doctor,
I'm afraid of the light.
You must be a bit dim.

Doctor, Doctor,
If you can't see me
now I'm leaving.
Calm down, what's wrong
with you?
I have a serious wait
problem.

Doctor, Doctor,
Everyone thinks I'm
invisible.
Who said that?

Jim: I keep seeing
fuzzy spots in front
of my eyes.
Sam: Have you seen
a doctor?
Jim: No just fuzzy spots.

Doctor, Doctor,
I keep thinking I look
like an Octopus.
How long has this been
on for?
Since I was a little squid.

Doctor, Doctor,
I'm losing my memory.
How long has this been
going on for?
How long has what
been going on from?

Doctor, Doctor,
I think I'm Donald
duck.
How long have these
Disney spells been
going on for?

Doctor, Doctor,
I swallowed your
surgeries clock.
Stop wasting my time!

When do doctors get angry?
When they've run out of patients!

Silly Space!

What did the alien
say to the tree?
Take me to your
cedar!

Hey did the earthling
fall in love with the
alien?
Because she was out
of this world.

How does the man
on the moon cut
his toenails?
Eclipse them.

How did the earthling
feel when an alien landed
with eight lasers for arms?
Stunned.

Knock, knock.
Who's there?
Cosmos.
Cosmos who?
Cosmos of us are
outside, you should
let us in!

How do you turn
a regular scientist
into a mad scientist?
Stand on her toes!

How do spacemen hold
up their pants?
With asteroid belts.

Knock, knock.
Who's there?
Apollo.
Apollo who?
Apollo-gize for not
answering sooner.

Silly Space!

Why did the atom
cross the road?
Because it was
time to split.

Why couldn't the
astronauts book a
room on the moon?
Because it was full.

Why wouldn't the
astronauts book a table
at the restaurant?
Because it had no
atmosphere!

Why did Captain Kirk
sneak into the ladies room?
Because ho wanted to go where no man
had gone before.

How does Darth Vader
know what you're getting
for Christmas?
He feels your presents.

What did the Sun
say when it was
introduced to the
earth?
Pleased to heat you.

What did the alien
say to the cat?
Take me to
your littler.

What robot always takes
the longest route?
R2 Detour.

Colour this Space page
in using only four colours,
and make it look amazing!

Cops n Robbers

What did the policeman say to his belly?
You're under a vest.

Did you hear about the sheep dog trials?
Two of the dogs we're found guilty.

A man rushed into a bank, then pointed his finger at the cashier, saying "This is a muck-up." 'Don't you mean stick-up'? said the cashier. 'No' said the man, 'muck-up I forgot my gun.

Knock, knock.
Who's there?
Irish stew.
Irish stew who?
Irish stew in the name of the law.

Where do policemen live?
Letsby Avenue.

What happened to man who stole a calendar?
He got twelve months.

The local wig shop was burgled last night, 200 wigs were stolen.
Police are now combing the area.

Policeman: Listen buddy this is a one way st.
Motorist: That's alright I'm only going one way.

Judge: What were you doing in the bank at 3 a.m. when the police entered?
Defendant: I was making a bolt for the door.

Silly Signs

CAUTION
THIS SIGN
HAS SHARP
EDGES

Warning
Please look under
your vehicles
for penguins

BEWARE
WILD ANIMALS/
CHILDREN

Wash & Vacum
Senior Citizens
£ 15.95

Not Responsible
if seagulls eat
your cake.

No Signs
Allowed!

Welcome
To
Accident

Silly Tongue Twisters

Try and do them all, then see if Mum and
Dad can do better.

I saw Susie sitting in a shoe shine shop.

Can you Can a can as a canner can can a can?

I scream, you scream, we all scream for Ice cream!

If two witches would watch two watches,
which witch would watch which watch?

Fuzzy Wuzzy was a bear. Fuzzy Wuzzy had
no hair. Fuzzy Wuzzy wasn't very Fuzzy, was he?

Round the rough and rugged rocked
the ragged rascal rudely ran.

I have got a date at quarter to eight;
I'll see you at the gate, so don't be late.

Peter Piper picked a peck of pickled peppers.
Did Peter Piper pick a peck of pickled peppers?
If Peter Piper picked a peck of pickled peppers,
where's the peck of
pickled peppers Peter Piper picked?

Tricky Tricks

They're harder than you think.
Ask Mum and Dad to watch.

Walk from one
side of the room
to the other, with
a book on your head.
If you can do this
gracefully you may
be related to Royalty!

Stand on one
leg blindfolded for
one minute.
If you can do
this you'll stop
wearing both shoes
out.

Stand perfectly still
for five minutes, you're
not allowed to laugh.
This is very difficult,
and you're very talented
if you succeed.

Juggle with three
balls.
If you can do this
you have superb
timing.

Eat three crackers
in a minute.
If you're a crummy
athlete, you'll find
this impossible.

Get from one side
of the room, to
the other on your
back with an apple
on your belly, all
the way.

Count to twenty
backwards without
pausing?
If you can do
this you're very clever.

Now it's Mum
and Dads turn, make sure they don't cheat.

Silly Weather

How do you
know if it's been
raining cats and
dogs?
When you step
in a poodle.

Why did the
lumberjack wear
a helmet?
It was raining
Cat's and Logs.

What did one
snowman say to
the other?
Do you smell
carrots?

Why isn't the sky
happy on clear
days?
Because it has
the blues.

How do hurricanes
see?
With one eye.

What is wind?
Air in a hurry.

Why is lightning
so naughty?
It doesn't know
how to conduct
itself.

What's a volcano?
A mountain with
hiccups.

What type of cloud
is so lazy it won't
get up?
Fog.

What do clouds
wear under their
clothes?
Thunderwear.

Man: What's the weather like outside?
Silly Billy: I don't know it's to foggy to see.

My Secrets

Only share with best friends
and Mum and Dad.

Don't tell a soul! *Don't tell a soul!*

What I'd like to be
when I grow up.

My favourite music.

Don't tell a soul!

The Boy/Girl
I want to marry.

What country
I want to live in.

Don't tell a soul!

Don't tell a soul!

What I like
to do in my spare
time.

Don't tell a soul!

My favourite colour.

My Secrets

Only share with best friends
and Mum and Dad.

My prayers.

My answered
prayers.

My favourite
tv program.

My favourite
films.

My favourite
animal.

My favourite
comedian.

Daft Jokes!

What was the crab sent to jail?
He kept on pinching things.

How did the police catch the strawberry thief?
They caught him red handed.

What's the safest way to hammer nails in?
Get your sister to hold the nails.

What's are the two strongest days of the week?
Saturday and Sunday, because the others are week days.

What goes ha-ha-ha-bonk?
A woman laughing her head off.

What's the difference between a baker and an elephant?
One bakes the bread, the other breaks the bed.

How do you wake a cockerel?
Set he's alarm cluck.

What does a baker have in common with a poor man?
They both knead some dough.

Sillly Poems

I once knew a Prince
too small
Who loved a Princess
Too tall
He grew sadder and
sadder
Until he found
a ladder
And took it along to
the ball.

Mr Krispell copyright

My Silly Poem

Write it below.

Dads Poem

Write Dad a lovely poem below.

Mums Poem

Write Mum a lovely poem below.

Silly Dinosaurs

What do you call
a dinosaur with
a limp?
My-foot-is-saurus.

What do you
call a dinosaur
who won't stop
talking about himself?
A dinobore.

Do dinosaurs
pass exams?
Yes, with extinction.

What do you call
a blind dinosaur?
Do-you-think-he-saw-us.

How do you
ask a dinosaur
to lunch?
Tea Rex?

What does a T-rex
eat?
Anything he wants.

What happened
to the smelly dinosaurs
They became Ex-stinked.

Why did dinosaurs
eat raw meat?
Because they didn't
know how to cook.

What followed the
dinosaurs?
Their tails.

What do you
call a very articulate
dinosaur?
A theraurus.

Where can you find a dinosaur in a bikini?
At the Dino-shore.

Colour this picture in for Dad!

For a
lovely Dad

Silly Elephants

Why do elephants
paint their toenails
red?
To hide in cherry
trees!

What's the loudest
noise in the
jungle?
Giraffes eating
from cherry trees!

How do you
know if there's an
elephant in your
bed?
You can see the
E on his pyjamas.

Why is an elephant
big grey and wrinkly?
Because if he was
small white and round
he'd be an aspirin.

What should you
give an elephant with
an upset stomach?
Plenty of room.

How do you
fit four elephants
in a mini?
Two in the
front and two
in the back?

How do you
get four monkeys
in a mini?
Ask the elephants
to got out first.

What do you
get if you cross
a mouse with
an elephant?
Big holes in
your skirting board.

If you had two
elephants in a mini
what game would
they be playing?
Squash!

What goes up slowly
and down quickly?
An elephant in
an elevator.

Funny Food

How do you reach
the top of an
ice cream mountain?
With a Jellycopter.

Why shouldn't you
tell an egg a joke?
It might crack up.

What do you call
two banana skins
on the floor?
A pair of slippers.

How can you
make a chicken stew?
Leave it waiting
for hours.

What happens when
you stand on
a grape?
It lets out
a little wine.

Which vegetable goes
best with a
jacket potato?
Button mushrooms.

What biscuit can
fly?
A plane one.

What are the two things
you can't have for
breakfast?
Lunch and supper.

Why did the jelly
wobble?
Because it saw
the milkshake.

Why was the
orange crying?
Because someone hurt
it's peelings.

How do you start a jelly race?
Ready, Set, Go!

Funny Food

Why was the
biscuit sad?
He felt crummy.

Why do all the
vegetables love
the mushroom?
Because he's a
fun-guy.

Why was the
Swiss Cheese praying?
Because he was hole-y.

Why was the small
strawberry crying?
His parents were
in a bit of a jam.

How don you know
of a hamburgers
married.
It wears an onion
ring.

Why was the biscuit
crying?
His mummy had
been a wafer so long.

Why did the plumb
go out with the
raisin.
Because she couldn't
find a date.

What day of the
week do sausages
hate?
Fryday!

What do Rice Krispies
we're on their feet?
Kelloggs.

How do you
make a banana
split?
Cut it in half.

What's yellow and stupid?
Thick custard.

Jump in the jellycopter
and count the candy in
the custard sea, with one
eye closed. Time 2 minutes.

Write the answers above.

Correct answer
Sweet 15
Candy cane 15
Ice cream 12

Daft Jokes

What did the loaf of bread, say to the knife?
You wanna piece of me?

Who one the fight between the bread and the knife?
The knife because the cake was a crummy fighter.

What happened to the rabbits that got married?
They went on a bunny-moon.

How did the two rabbits get back from their bunny-moon.
They caught a plane from the hareport.

What do you get if a bear catches you with a honey jar?
A very sticky situation.

What do get if you cross a crazy hippo with a dessert?
A hippo-potty-mousse

Why do French people eat snails?
Because they don't like fast food.

What do you call a piano with only white keys?
A minor problem.

Dad have you got a good memory?
Yes son, why do you ask?
I've just smashed your shaving mirror.

Ask Mum to help you colour this in.

For Grandad
and Grandma.

Our Family Jokes

Write your own favourite family jokes!

Dads

Mums

Grandmas

Grandpas

Brothers

Sisters

Aunts

Uncles

Silly Insects!

What did the fly
say as it hit
the windscreen?
That's me all over.

What's the last
thing that goes
through a wasps
mind when it hits
a windscreen?
It's sting.

Did you hear
about the two
silk worms that
had a race?
It ended in
a tie.

What's the difference
between a bird and
a fly?
A bird can fly but
a fly can't bird.

What's the difference
between school dinners
a slugs?
School dinners come
on a plate.

How do fleas
travel long distance?
By itch hiking.

Why were the flies
playing soccer on a
saucer?
They were practicing
for the cup.

What insect never
leaves you alone?
A stick insect.

Why don't baby
birds smile?
Would you if
your mother fed
you worms all day.

Why did the fly fly?
Because the spider spied her.

Silly Insects!

Where did the spider
meet his wife?
On a website.

What do you get
if you cross an
insect with a
baby?
A creepy crawler.

What does a cat
sleep on?
A catterpillow.

What's worse than
finding a worm
in your apple?
Finding half
a worm.

First cat: Where have
all those fleas gone?
Second cat: Search me.

What do moths
study at school?
Mothomatics.

What was the
snail doing on the
motorway?
A couple of miles
a week.

Where do bees
go when injured?
Waspital.

How do you tell
if a worm is a
boy or a girl?
Tell it a joke-
if he laughs it's
a boy, and if
she laughs it's
a girl.

What has four
wheels and flies?
A garbage truck.

Did you hear about the
man ran a successful flea circus?
He started from scratch.

Hidden ladybirds

 Find the Eight hidden ladybirds, then colour the picture in for Mum & Dad.

My Favourite Things!

(And I'm not joking)

Write the reasons why!

Mum

Dad

Best friend

2nd Best friend

3rd Best friend

Best Teacher

2nd Best Teacher

If I Ruled The World!

(And I'm not still joking)

Write what you'd do.

Day 1 I'd

Day 2 I'd

Day 3 I'd

Day 4 I'd

Day 5 I'd

Now take a rest you've just changed the world.

Now it's time for Dad to change the world.

Day 1 I'd

Day 2 I'd

Day 3 I'd

Day 4 I'd

Day 5 I'd

Now Dad's running the world, it's a great time to ask for an increase in pocket money!

Silly riddles!

What's bigger when it's upside down?

The number 6

What has a mouth, and a fork, but never eats?

A river.

What has a tail and a head but no body?

A coin.

How many side has a circle got?

Two- the inside and the outside.

What's in the middle of Paris?

The letter R.

What's black when it's clean and
white when it's dirty?

A blackboard.

What starts with t, ends with t and is
full of tea?

A teapot.

What asks no questions but demands
an answer?

A doorbell.

Jokes to tell your
Best Friend

How do eggs
leave in an emergency?
Through the fire eggsit.

What type of
nuts always have
a cold?
Cashews!

What do birds
watch on tv?
Duckumentaries!

What birds can
you find in Portugal?
Potu-geese!

What's the most
slippery country
in the world?
Greece!

Teacher: What is
a smoke detector
used for?
To tell Mum dinners
ready.

What do sea
monsters eat?
Fish and chips.

How do we
know that the
Earth won't come
to and end?
Because it's round.

How do crabs
call their friends?
On shell phones.

Where do you
find giant snails?
On the end of a
giants fingers.

What's higher than a giraffe?
A giraffes hat.

Jokes to tell your Best Friend

Did you hear about the Dutch women with inflatable shoes?
She popped her clogs.

I can make you talk like a Red Indian.
How?
See I told you.

Doctor, doctor I feel like a bridge.
What's come over you?
Well, so far two lorries, three cars and a bus.

What's snakes favourite subject?
Hiss-story.

Why was Beethoven's fifth favourite fruit?
Ba-na-na-na!

Shall I tell you the joke about the empty house?
There's nothing in it.

Why couldn't the skeleton go to the dance?
He had nobody to go with.

Why is six afraid of seven?
Because seven eight nine!

What's the best way to get straight A's?
Use a ruler.

For my
best friend

Silly School!

Teacher: If I have four apples in one hand and six in the other hand what do I have?
Pupil: Very big hands miss.

Teacher: I hope I didn't see you copy in that test?
Pupil: I hope you didn't, either.

Pupil: I don't think I deserved zero for the school test, sir.
Teacher: Neither do i, but it's the lowest I can give you.

Why was the chicken sent home from school?
For using fowl language.

Teacher: What do you know about Camelot?
Pupil: It's a parking area in the dessert.

Teacher: How did you get that black eye?
Pupil: You see that tree in the playground?
Teacher: Yes.
Pupil: I didn't.

Teacher: What does it mean when the smoke alarm goes off?
Pupil: At this school it means dinners ready.

Teacher: How do you spell education?
Pupil: E-D-U-A-Y-S-H-U-N.
Teacher: That's not how the dictionary spells it.
Pupil: You didn't ask me how the dictionary spells it.

Silly School!

Teacher: If I have four apples in one hand and six in the other hand what do I have?
Pupil: Very big hands miss.

Teacher: I hope I didn't see you copy in that test?
Pupil: I hope you didn't, either.

Pupil: I don't think I deserved zero for the school test, sir.
Teacher: Neither do i, but it's the lowest I can give you.

Why was the chicken sent home from school?
For using fowl language.

Teacher: What do you know about Camelot?
Pupil: It's a parking area in the dessert.

Teacher: How did you get that black eye?
Pupil: You see that tree in the playground?
Teacher: Yes.
Pupil: I didn't.

Teacher: What does it mean when the smoke alarm goes off?
Pupil: At this school it means dinners ready.

Teacher: How do you spell education?
Pupil: E-D-U-A-Y-S-H-U-N.
Teacher: That's not how the dictionary spells it.
Pupil: You didn't ask me how the dictionary spells it.

Silly School!

A boy walked into the school library and said, 'Fish and chips, please.' 'I'm sorry, but this is a library.' 'Sorry,' whispered the pupil, 'Fish and chips please.'

Pupil: Our dog bit four people yesterday so we had to have him put down.
Teacher: Was he mad?
Pupil: Well, he wasn't very happy.

Teacher: Can you tell me what language is spoken in Corsica?
Pupil: Course I can.

Teacher: Mrs Brown, I asked you to come in to discuss Sammy's appearance.
Mrs Brown: Why what's wrong with his appearance?
Teacher: He hasn't made one in my classroom since September.

Teacher: What two days begin with T?
Pupil: Today and tomorrow.

Teacher: Sammy, when's your birthday?
Sammy: May 12th.
Teacher: Which year?
Sammy: Every year.

Pupil: My bird died of flu yesterday?
Teacher: You poor thing, was it bird flu?
Pupil: No, he flew into a car.

Why do magicians do so well in school? They're good at trick questions.

Silly Jokes for Dad

(Don't tell them when Dad's watching sport)

Who's the most wanted criminal in the ocean?
Al Caprawn.
(A shellfish criminal)

Who's the second most wanted criminal in the ocean?
Billy the Squid.

(He robbed the riverbank)

Dad: I'm thinking of getting a pig and keeping it in your room?
Teenager: But what about the smell?
Dad: The pig will just have to get used to it.

How do you burn a Silly Billy on the ear?
Phone him up when he's ironing.

Diner: Can I have an elephant sandwich please?
Waiter: I'm sorry, sir, we've run out of bread.

What goes snap, crackle?
Two Rice Krispies.

Passenger: Why has this train stopped?
Guard: We hit a cow, madam.
Passenger: was it on the track?
Guard: No we had to chase it across a field.

Police arrested two men yesterday, one for drinking battery acid, and one for eating fireworks.
They charged one and let off the other.

Silly Jokes for Dad

(Don't tell them when Dad's watching sport)

What do you get
if you drop a
piano down a coal
mine?
A flat minor.

First man: How many
people work in
your office?
Second man: About
half of them.

What's
black and shoots
out of the ground
shouting knickers?
Crude oil.

What
black and shoots
out of the ground
shouting pants?
Refined oil.

Son: Why haven't you
spoke to Mum all
week?
Dad: Well, son, I don't
like to interrupt her.

Why do bakers
work so hard?
Because they need
the dough.

Patient: Doctor, my hair
is falling out, is there
something you can give
me for it?
Doctor: Ask at reception,
they'll give you a box.

Last night a gigantic
whole suddenly appeared
in the middle of the road.
Don't worry council
workers are looking
into it.

Silly Jokes for Mum

(Don't tell these when Dad's around)

Mum: Dad tried to take me out last night, in a car with wooden doors, wooden wheels, and even a wooden engine.
Son: How was the drive?
Mum: I don't know, it wooden go.

What happened to the snail who lost his shell?
He became very sluggish.

What do you get hanging from banana trees?
Sore arms.

Mum: Dad had a terrible dream last night that he was eating a giant marshmallow?
Son: Whats so terrible about that?
Mum: When he awoke his pillow was missing.

Son: What happens when a car is too clapped out and old to work?
Mum: Someone sells it to Dad.

Where do frogs get there eyes tested?
At the hopician.

What happened when the Granny Smith married the Cox's pipin?
They lived appley ever after.

Son: Dad, will you do my English homework for me tonight?
Dad: No, son, it wouldn't be right.
Son: Well, just do your best.

Son: Mum, Dad says I got my intelligence from him.
Mum: He must be right I've still got mine.

What do you call?

What do you call a girl with a frog on her head?
Lilly.

What do you call a man sitting on your doormat?
Bill.

What do you call a woman with a weight on one side
of her head?
Eileen.

What do you call a man with a spade on his head?
Doug.

What do you call a man without a spade on his head?
Douglas.

What do you call a nun with a washing machine on her head?
Sister-matic.

What do you call a man with a loo on his head?
John.

What do you call a woman with two toilets on her head?
Lulu.

What do you call a woman who stands astride a river?
Bridget.

What do you call a man with no legs?
Neil.

What do you call?

What do you call a cow with two leg?
Lean beef.

What do you call a man floating in the sea?
Bob.

What do you call a deer with no eyes?
No idea.

What do you call a dear with no eyes and no legs?
Still no idea.

What do you call a women who slides
around on a piece of bread?
Marge.

What do you call a man with a jack on his Head?
Jack.

What do you call a man who dunks his
head into his tea?
Duncan.

Why do you call a woman with a tortoise on her head?
Shelly.

What do you call a man with a bag of compost on his head?
Pete.

Silly Monsters!

Did you hear about the monster who cleaned the attic with his girlfriend? Now he can't get the cobwebs out of her fur.

How do you keep a big ugly monster in suspense? I'm not telling you!

Why wouldn't the small zombie go to school? He felt rotten.

Why did King Kong eat Big Ben? Because it was time for lunch.

Why did Cyclops give up teaching? He only had one pupil.

What monster lives in a tree? Frank-in-pine.

Where do monsters go to party? To a Scooby-Dooby-Doo.

What monster always rings the doorbell? The Knock-less-monster.

Why did the Fungi Monster have so many friends? Well, he kind of grew on you in the end.

I dined with a monster I knew
So proud of his big pot of goo
Carrots and bats
Ferrets and rats
I spent the next week on the loo

See if you can copy this sketch.

Silly Birthday's

What did the
little candle say
to the big candle?
You're too young
to go out.

How can you
tell that birthdays
are good for you?
Because people who
live the longest tend
to have the most
birthdays

What did the clam
do on his birthday?
He shellybrated.

What has long wings,
a long tail and wears
a bow?
A birthday Pheasant.

What do you get
every birthday?
A year older.

What do you
call an adult balloon?
A blown-up.

Son: Dad what's the
easiest way to remember
mums birthday?
Dad: Forget it once.

What if no one comes
to your birthday party?
You can have your cake
and eat it.

Where can you find
a great birthday present
for a cat?
In a Cat-alogue.

Were any famous men
born on your birthday?
No only babies.

What do you call a crazy balloon?
A balloonatic.

Balloonatic

What crazy balloon escaped from
The balloonatic asylum?

Silly Snow!

What do snowmen wear
on their heads?
Ice caps.

What do snowmen
call their offspring?
Chill-dren.

Where do snowmen go
to dance?
To Snowballs.

Wear Did Jack Frost
meet his wife?
On the winter-net.

How does a snowman
get to work?
By icicle.

Where do snowmen
keep their money?
In the snowbank.

What kind of money
do snowmen use?
Ice lolly.

What did the executioner
say to his mother?
Only twenty chopping
days to Christmas.

Why is an armchair
like a Christmas dinner?
Because it's full off
stuffing.

What side of a Robin
has the most
feathers?
The outside.

Silly Riddles

What's hidden in the pictures?

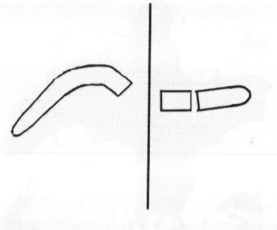

A worm crossing over a razor blade.

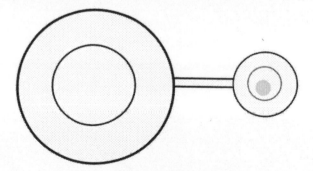

A Mexican frying a egg.

Silly Riddles

What's hidden in the pictures?

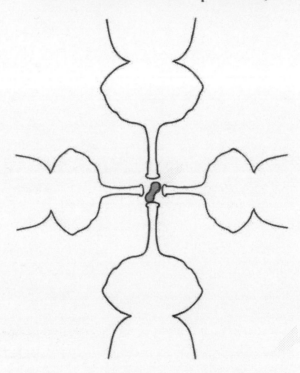

Four Elephants tying to e a peanut.

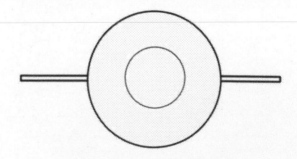

A Mexican riding a bike.

Silly Princess

Cinderella: Oh Dear
the ugly sisters fell
down the wishing well
last night?
Prince: I didn't know
wishing wells worked!

Why did Snow White
treat all dwarfs
equally?
Because she was
the fairest of
all of them.

What did the
prince sing to
the mermaid?
'Salmond-enchanted-
evening!

Why did Pinocchio
leave Cinderella?
Because he said she
was just stringing
him along.

Why was Snow White
thrown out of the
soccer team ?
She kept on running
away from the ball.

Prince: Ugly sister
why is your nose
so swollen?
Ugly sister: I was
smelling a brose.
Prince: There no B
in brose.
Ugly sister: There was
in this one.

What did Cinderella's
fish wear to
the ball?
Glass flippers.

What did the
seven dwarfs sing
whilst working in
the butchers?
Gristle while you
work.

Daft jokes!

Where on a ship
do you find sailors
laughing?
Where the funnel be!

When were there
only three vowels in
the alphabet?
A long time ago,
before U and I
born.

What cows live
in the North Pole?
Friesian cows.

Where can you grow
space carrots?
In force fields.

What do you
call a nude man
on a high wire?
A tension-seeker.

Where does an
iron live?
With his flat mates.

Why do you
call a duck that
goes Bang! Then lights
up the sky?
A firequaker.

Why was the
frog sent to
jail?
He Kermited a crime.

What's the first words a
baby computer says?
Data!

Thank you for
purchasing this book.
If you enjoyed it
please give it
a review!

Printed in the United States of America

First Printing, 2018

Contact. Sniffitysnoo302@gmail.com

I can highly recommend...

Mr Krispell's Kids Joke Book!

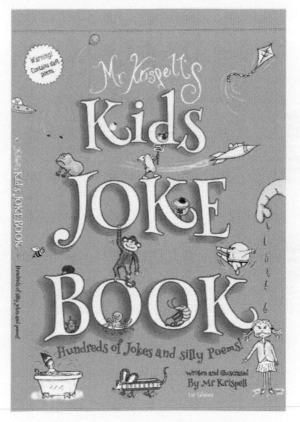

What's got big ears, a tail and
squeaks when you blow into it?
A Mouse-organ!
Mr Krispell's Kids Joke Book
contains hundreds of new jokes,
classic jokes and hilariously
daft poems, wonderfully illustrated.

Made in the USA
Columbia, SC
21 January 2019